ABOUT THE AUTHOR

Enigmatic. Mysterious. Drenched in Shadow. **Josie Alford** is none of these things. Her stage presence is sequinned, pop culture referencing, infectious, & welcoming. Once seen, never forgotten, her work ranges from the subtle nuance of dealing with loss to Spice Girls fan mail.

Josie Alford is a Bristol-based poet, YouTuber and award winning reviewer. Her poetry fuses the techniques of spoken and written poetry. Having completed an MA in Creative Writing at Bath Spa, she has since produced her debut poetry collection about the death of her father.

"Josie Alford is one of the new wave of spoken word performers; sassy, intelligent young women who knock the gatekeepers of 'proper poetry' off their dusty pedestals." - Lucy English

Josie Alford
Faulty Manufacturing

VERVE
POETRY PRESS
BIRMINGHAM

PUBLISHED BY VERVE POETRY PRESS
https://vervepoetrypress.com
mail@vervepoetrypress.com

FIRST PUBLISHED MAR 2023

Printed and bound in the UK
by ImprintDigital, Exeter

ISBN: 978-1-913917-32-6

Cover Illustration by Anna-Louise Highley

For Izzy and James
and all the members of Dead Parent Club

CONTENTS

Acknowledgements & Credits

Faulty Manufacturing

Widemouth Bay

pronounced WID-muth

There was the swell,
the sets kept coming
there was no one there to surf them,

the man who had a family
on these cliffs, who held feasts
and raised cans in praise of the waves,
was gone.

The sand shared its memories
of cigarette butts and handmade surfboards.
The sea remembered sunrise surfing
and sunsets with green flashes.
The cliffs spoke of chess games
and all-night parties.

I sit, as I always have,
studying the sea
which perpetually throws itself back
towards me.

Bedtime Story, 2001

I worked in IT but lived
for the weekend. I'd pack a van
full of friends and boards and booze,

set off for the coast every Friday afternoon.
We surfed every sunrise and every night
headed into Bude to drink. Rinse and repeat.

After one such night of revelling
we went for our standard end-of-the-night
kebab and got chatting to some local girls.

One of them had lost an earring:
Trust me, I'm a Doctor, Uncle Rich said.
He worked in Sainsbury's.
When I told them so, the tall one laughed.

I saw your mother for the first time:
her eyes reminded me of the sea.

Our Kitchen Table

It stood in the epicentre of our family:
perforated with grooves that were once
growth-rings of a living Oak.

Between seismic coffee circles,
wine stains and cigarette burns,
glitter sat in the cracks.

Now some nights we stay up late,
pull the kitchen light down low,
draw in from the night,
sip whiskey and tell tales.

We got you second hand,
sometimes I wonder
how many families you held up;
how many romantic evenings you hosted,
how many postcards,
bills and bank statements you read.
I marvel at the fault lines
you held together at dinner.

Glossop Ward

In the hospital bed my father sagged
and bulged in all the wrong places,
his face awkward with frailty.

He said the nebuliser smelled like French bakeries
so I emptied Waitrose of its pastries
and drove them to him.

The next day he changed his T-shirt.
I pulled the blue concertina curtains
and saw my father for the first time:

arms and shoulders; bones with skin too big—
belly and wrists swollen
from lack of trying.

Soon, he managed to shower, glowed brighter
made plans for moving closer,
promised to call.

When he was discharged, I drove home,
my car full of the scent of a freshly baked start.

Filton, Autumn

Across tilted football pitches,
the sparrows are relentless:
they strive to say that nature still lives,
she will be heard.

The school run carnival passes
with babbling languages.
The beeches and sycamores eek out the last
of this year's colour and the sun plummets
with all the speed of a thrown tennis ball.

As grinning dogs race through puddles,
fireworks toast the thickening dark.

We are the Fire Starters

For James

Huddled over the communal barbecue
we take the embers of a dying warmth,
add kindling and well-placed charcoal.

You give long, slow, deep breaths.
I asked where you learnt
to feed fire like I do.

Dad

was leader of Cubs and taught you then
that fires need fuel, oxygen, heat;
as long as you keep breathing,
the flames will continue to grow.

A Smoker at a Bus Stop

It had been a long night.
She rolled a cigarette; distributed
tobacco evenly, placed
the filter in the right end, tucked
the corners in, licked, turned
it closed.

You should give that up you know.

It had been a long night.
She rolled her eyes, distributed
her weight evenly, placed
the cigarette in her mouth, tucked
the corners of her mouth into a smile, turned.
Really? Why?

They're bad for you, mind,
those things will kill you.

Corsham Court

If a motorcycle dare raise its voice
the air forces it into submissive silence.
But it doesn't seem to mind the birds,

cheeping and chirping, chiffing and chaffing,
they chant in the arms of ancient beeches.
The pumpkin spiced leaves crunch and crack

under damp trainers.
I close my eyes, and as the wind rushes
through the tree's swirling limbs

my hair whips and whirls
to the song. I hear the sea;
The ocean breathes from its belly,

exhales saline breeze,
withdraws across the clicking pebbles
only to rush forward once more.

I breathe out and open my eyes,
with the sea still singing in my ears.

December the Twentieth

after Don DeLillo

1

There was blood,
his blood, on the tissue in his hand.

The smoke he'd made was there,
He didn't know where his cigarette was.
He slept.

He dreamt he could see straight
out over the ocean, which,
if he was not mistaken,
was through the wall to his right.

He woke,
his breath came in short bursts.
His lungs were falling away
to be replaced by bile.

A star was out, he watched it.
He tried the breathing exercises;
short puffs.

A lack of air, pain, blood,
He watched the star blink and move
before part of his lung
came loose and blocked an artery.

2

The floor slid beneath his daughter
knees up, head between them.
There was a policeman
at the end of his night shift
trying not to yawn on the phone.

They had found him
and would take him away.
His landlady had already burnt the bed.

It was forever and impossible
When it was done, she got up,
stood among the fragile cups—
a mandala of inconsequential things,
and dialled numbers. She spoke.
There were voices in her ear,
in the empty room, one then another
in tearful echo,
mourning in the guise of speech.

I'm sorry.
He's dead.
I'm sorry.

There was the smell of something
familiar. She could not find herself.
In her hand, she saw a lit cigarette.

Corsham Court, After

There is no wind today, no breeze
to call me home, no leaves
for it to rustle anyway,

just fog, muffled and heavy.
There is nothing to silence
the distant roar of traffic.

The same beech has no song to sing.
Its branches wordlessly criss-cross
cages on the grey-white sky.

My trainers are damp
from whispering trails of green
footprints in the silver-tipped grass.

I miss the sea.
It would not stand
for being this still or quiet.

On the steps of this old house
surrounded by broken branches,
it has never felt so far away.

Silence Learning to Live with Itself

The silence has forgotten how to speak.
It does not know how to articulate its feelings
so has given up on talking altogether.

The silence dwells in forgotten cups of tea.
It throws its cigarette butts over the garden hedge,
hoping the neighbours don't see,
it tries not to bother anyone.

The silence can't sleep
no matter how much it drinks.
The silence wakes up hungover,
the silence hates itself.

The silence brushes awkwardly
against itself in the hallway.
It watches TV, tries to get comfortable,
makes itself small on the sofa.

The silence grows to accommodate
its disquieted mind.
It tries mindfulness
to release pressure.
Nothing stops the relentless noise.

Portrait of a Father from Memory

He could have been 5'11" if he didn't slouch,
this was the cause or effect
of needing a hip replacement. After drinking
the slouch became more pronounced.

He was never very large but his last years
stole the meat from his bones and left
his skin baggy. His clothes
looked the same way, old T-shirts
hung on pointed shoulders. His jeans
were held up by a belt, creased
with a timeline of tighter holes.

His knuckles— too big and covered
in scars. Yellow nails— too thick to cut,
gathered dirt willingly.

His hair was salt and pepper
ugly; the same as his beard— unplanned,
and untrimmed. It hid his paper skin.

His smile used to be beautiful
but his teeth grew almost black,
pointed in all sorts of directions,
his gums were bleached.
His eyes were weak
watery blue bloodshot
and stared out from under eyebrows
that hung forward and flicked upwards
like Grandad's.

In the end, his face was dying:
all fight had left his eyes
months ago, around the time
he stopped getting out of bed,
and started pouring his drinks a little stronger.

New Year's Eve

At midnight,
I called you:

I was worried,
you were alone.

It took two
0.4-second tones

'til I realised
you had died.

It carried on,
the audible ring,

the answerphone
never existed.

I was left on stone steps with the dial tone
and the crackle of other people's fireworks.

If my Father's Answerphone Worked

Hey it's me—
Call me back.

Hey it's me—
Your landlady called;
said you couldn't breathe.
Have you been taking your meds?
Call me.

Hey it's me—
How did it go at the doctors?
Call me if you need
anything.
Love you.

Hey it's me—
I'm on my way to the hospital.
See you soon.

Hey—
Granny called;
said she hasn't spoken to you in weeks,
come to think of it,
I can't remember when we last spoke.

My Father's Crocs

See how they are spattered white,
it could be paint or ash or
something unknowable.

See how the hinge is stuck
like a door to a tomb or
some forgotten place.

Here, the plastic has faded
like a plaque on a bench by the sea,
someone loved it here.

See how they are worn
down like a coast path, eroding.
She told us he died in them.

We tried to leave them behind
but here they are; right where she left them—
falling apart
on the front step of our family home.

Tuberculosis as an Unwanted Companion

Apparently, It had been following my father
for a while, but encouraged by his lifestyle,
It made its presence known a year before It killed him.

He played It down on the phone
but It had already added us on Facebook,
insisted his children come to visit.

It sat us on an unfamiliar sofa that couldn't fit us,
made us tea and cake, encouraged us
to talk while It sat in an armchair and watched.

It eavesdropped on our increasingly rare
phone calls, It was the crackle on the line
and It hung in the back of every word.

It was there at the hospital, curled up
on his chest and wrapped around his neck,
It did not like the nebuliser.

It wavered on the edge of offense,
never quite saying enough to illicit
anger— I held my tongue.

On the day It killed him,
instead of leaving It stuck around,
hung in the air in his room, the smell of his clothes.

It was there at the funeral;
It got drunk and danced around the room
while everyone tried to ignore It.

On Clearing My Father's Belongings

After Philip Larkin

This was your room, your hired box,
until recently. Nicotine-stained
curtains lay open to the way
across the hills to distant moors.

He just had so much crap, we can burn
most of it for you if you want she said.
The bed had already gone. But we each kept
some small tokens; I took

novelty mugs, and the brand new
unused hoover; Izzy sorted through
laptops, tablets, and phones; James took
clothes that fit, and the games never played.

We sold what we could and threw the rest away.
I'd have liked to have left it there;
let the dust make a home;
let rows of shoes, quiet blank screens,

the overflowing ashtray made from an old can,
mismatched furniture and chairs stacked
with unread letters and the boxes of pills
you never took, stand

as the measure of what was left of your life.
But it had to go, your landlady wanted it
empty, wanted her guest room back.

An Awfully Big Adventure

The last time it snowed in Devon
my Father piled his landlady, her boyfriend,
her daughter and my brother into his
ramshackle van and set off for Dartmoor.
They sledged all afternoon on bin lids,
recycling bags and dinner trays.

The next day, in his cleverness,
he bought three sledges for his three children
and waited for the snow to come back.

After he had been put into boxes,
we found years of lost boy's toys
gathering damp.

Broken remote control helicopters,
power kites, an inflatable kayak
and three unused sledges.

When the snow finally came, and the country
stopped under it all, I sold them
to a beaming man whose son had never seen snow before.

Uneven Road

The last time I drove you
was the weekend before you died.
We'd already pulled over once
for you to hack and wretch up lumps
to decay at the side of the road.

When we got to that certain stretch
between Okehampton
and Sourton Down
before the A30, I accelerated—
bump bump bump
I did it on purpose—
    bump
knew that you too would feel
the unpleasant rise and fall—
     bump
I knew it would make you worse—
      bump
and I wanted it to—
    bump
you deserved it—
   bump
after everything.
  bump

Today, I am driving home
for the first time since your funeral.
I accelerate.
bump bump bump.

Faulty Manufacturing

Not at the beginning, but later on, something broke, which might never have been made right in the first place. I remember in patches. Father was not a nice man, liked his drink, got carried away by it. He was a violent man. At least that is how I remember it. Sunday night. School tomorrow. Dragged out of bed by my hair past my sister— asleep or pretending to be. Mum wasn't there, I can't remember why. I had school tomorrow. He smelled of Stella, cheap whisky and stale fag smoke. At the funeral, they fondly remembered the rollies, one always hanging from his lower lip. When I told him I had school tomorrow, something about SATs or GCSEs, he slapped me. Lifted me up by my neck against the microwave. Mum would be mad if the washing up wasn't done. Once. I told her. She confronted him, I was there. He dragged his empty suitcase, slapped it down in the living room and pointed and screamed *Every time you talk like this I want to pack my bags and go* and stared us down. *Well fucking go then.* I spoke calmly. I shouted. I didn't say anything at all but wished I had. I remember in patches. Later. Walking him home from the local down miles of black-bile-lanes, I carried the weight of him, held him up while he pissed on our shoes. Another time, I wasn't there. He fell. Broke his nose on the ice. It sat a smidge to the left, his left, ever since. *Do you remember any of this?* In a way, I knew I'd never know. Later. On the phone, he spat *There's a reason why I drink.* I hung up—starting a pattern of clicks and dial tones that shaped our remaining years. On days like this in a life I have built for myself I wear my hair short, tuck rollies behind my ears and in the corners of my mouth. I sip cheap whisky and remember in patches.

One Day I Woke Up and I Realised that God is Dead

1

It was more a slow unravelling;
God started dying when I was nine:
my Dad would not go to heaven
because my Heavenly Father wouldn't let him
if he didn't apologise for everything—
they were both too stubborn.

2.

A boy at Sunday School told me
that Mum was going to hell too
because of the divorce, God faded
behind the fear-soaked reality at home.
He shrugged, told me that marriage vows
are for life. Injustice
burnt behind my eyes,
inside my furious mouth.

3.

Then came the questions
Each one a loose thread
I wanted to stop pulling:
Is God a homophobe?
                Does he hate women,
or is that just the church
                    and the men who run it?
Why does God advocate an eye-for-an-eye punitive justice
system in the Old Testament but a live-and-let-live
rehabilitative system in the New Testament?

Did he change his mind
                 because he realised that
he was wrong?
          Can God be wrong?
                 Did he always intend
it this way and set up all those people to fail?
                    Is God an arsehole?

4.

One day I woke up and God had gone,
stolen away in the night leaving nothing
but loss— the absence of a thing.
I knew fear for the first time: Death
meant something, or rather it meant
nothing.

At the centre of this swirling
tangled uncertainty was a knot
I did not want to look at.

He never existed in the first place.

There was no woven plan–
there was nothing.
The nothing was huge.
It had been here
all along.

Grief Cycle

You would have been fifty-five today
and I'm finishing off the litre of Whyte & Mackay
I bought you four days before you died. I bought it
because you asked me to.

The first time I grieved for you, Father, you
were at the bottom of Mum's stairs,
head held in shaking hands.
It was not the first time I'd seen you cry,
but the first time you'd failed us.

Then there was every cigarette
you rolled around your tuberculosis
tucked with the knowledge
you were not taking your meds.

After you died, I had to pick the music
for your funeral and realised I had no idea
what you liked.

It is all just a collection of moments that take
your stomach in their fist and twist
for a second, for days, for a few minutes
until you shake yourself free and carry on.

Now, sometimes, I pedal too fast
to feel the wind rip tears
from my eyes. All the time
knowing you taught me to do this
and I realise that half
the grieving started before you died.

An Exercise in How to Move On

I find running helps,
it feels like halfway between positive and punishing.

Recently the past has been catching up.
I've been pounding Filton pavements
round the back of the MOD, to Asda and back
in unsupportive footwear, telling myself
that sanity lies in a 10-minute mile
that I just can't reach when I've been
smoking the tobacco you left behind,

there's the first 10k; I was running high
all endorphins round the harbourside
but the beers necked in celebration smell of you,

it doesn't last,
I end up blistered,
at night, I tighten and ache,
my hips scream, knees burn, ankles cry,
but my brain finally stops running, lies quiet, and sleeps

which I guess
is all I wanted.

April the Eighteenth

Dear Dad,
Today, I miss you.

I keep thinking about all the things
that are going wrong and I know
that you'd have been able to fix it.

All I'd have to do is call you mid-morning,
both of us at work, and hope
you hadn't started that first can
of Stella; before your syllables
became blurred and you randomly
paused mid-sentence because you forgot
I was there.

When you were sober, I learnt so much.
You had knowledge on the most
hodge-podge things.
You'd listen to me too, would want to learn
about my day and hear the latest thing
I'd written. You wouldn't like
what I've written recently. You'd probably
hang up and never talk to me again.
So I guess it's better that you can't

but—
today I miss you.
I just want to hear your fucking laugh
and the click and hiss of a can being opened.

Charity Shop Clear Out

My house is full of boxes
of your stuff, but instead
I cleared out my wardrobe:
threw out the bits that didn't fit or feel right.

I kept two Christmas jumpers—
one for family, the other
says *Merry Go Fuck Yourself*
you would have liked it.

I threw out the shirt
with that wine stain that I never
managed to get out.

I kept the T-shirt you bought me
from the surf shop, it had a sunrise
on the front and cost a fiver. But,
I grew out of the wetsuit years ago,
having only worn it once.

I did it to make room, to make space
because my wardrobe feels too crowded—
the hallway fills with our discarded selves.

Something To Dream About

For Izzy

Do you remember when we shared a room?
We had separate sides and separate CD players:
you played Busted and I played McFly,
but we both loved *Air Hostess,*
Obviously.

Do you remember *Everytime?*
We'd sing Britney, full-lunged,
our beds one on top of the other,
performing to the ceiling
until we were shouted into silence.

Do you remember Blankie?
The red, green, grey, crocheted best friend.
I still have Princess.
She sits still on my pillows,
watching over my room when I'm gone,
I still whisper secrets to her.

Do you remember dreaming?
You never struggled to sleep
but I sometimes needed help
so I'd ask for something to dream about.
You'd ask for my favourite colour,
which was mostly always purple,
and tell me to dream of a purple world.

So I did:
the walls and floors— purple,
the sky and clouds— purple.
There was a purple you and a purple me—
Mcfly wore purple too.
We only ate purple broccoli and aubergines.
We drank Ribena, ate grape flavoured sweets,
and smelled of Parma Violets.

I need something to dream about again.
Because my memories are dropping
like old post-its and
I write and write
and stick and stick
but they still manage to peel away.

The Vernacular of Human Resources

1

Someone complained about me at work
so HR in its infinite wisdom
got me to do a personality strength test
in the hope that I learn to work better with others.

My first strength is Strategy:
apparently, I'm good at making decisions.
HR asked me if any decision I'd made
had turned out less than perfect:
agreeing to this was certainly a mistake, I thought.
No, I said,
*but depends on your philosophical definition
of perfection*, I added.

My second strength is Communication:
apparently, I'm good at talking to people,
hosting, and writing. Honestly, I was pleased
until, according to the branded laminated
flash cards, I can talk too much and don't listen.
This is when I stopped listening.

My third strength is Woo:
I shit you not—
apparently, it stands for Winning Others Over
it's Manipulation's prettier sister in a dress.
for me, there are no strangers— only friends
I haven't influenced yet.

My fourth strength is Learner:
apparently, I learn the basic knowledge
but nothing in depth or worth knowing.

My fifth strength is Activator:
apparently, I start things but rarely finish them.
The word "superficial" was bandied around a lot.

2

I need your advice, Dad, because shockingly,
of all the qualities I inherited from you,
I didn't get your ability to understand
this sort of nonsense; because right now,
I'm in a place where I can turn my strengths
into reasons why I'm a sociopath and I need you.
I need you to tell me that some HR mumbo jumbo
fuckery pseudo-science made to keep the workforce
compliant and productive did not completely suss me.

Fathers' Day in the Mixed Unreal Conditional

I am writing alternate histories and hypothetical futures
you moved closer to us like you said you would
out of isolation and into your family
maybe I would have seen you today
popped round and cooked or taken you out
a nice roast
maybe I would have bought you a tie
or something else equally pointless
out of some misplaced sense of obligation
because you're here
you're my dad
because I should

you didn't move
stayed hiding in a friend's garage
maybe I would have sent you a card
carefully selected one without a booze-related joke
maybe I would have called you
maybe you would have picked up
and we could have talked
and I would have told you that I feel numb
like I'm not here at all
like I'm watching my life creep away
like it's on a TV screen and I'm somewhere else
maybe I'd have asked if you ever felt like this

maybe I wouldn't feel this way at all
wouldn't feel like the soles peel off my trainers
and everything falls out when I think about calling you

maybe you would be there on some future Mothers' Day
maybe you would have baby-proofed yourself
smoothed out your hard edges
put your toxic ingredients in a jar out of reach
maybe you would have sought help
so that we could be a proper family
like we always tried to be

maybe seeing the love in your eyes
would have healed me too
would have put my fears in a box under the bed
where I could find my own hard edges if I needed to

this will do me no good
your ashes are in a cardboard box
on a shelf
ninety-eight miles away

Father of the Bride

I'm ashamed to say I'm glad
he won't be there:
I won't have to carry him

down the aisle
a shuffling, drunken past.
He won't be there

to slur through his speech.
I won't have to worry
about what he might do.

He won't be there
to ruin it, except,
in his absence.

August the Fourteenth

Buildings hurl themselves at the sand
on the other side of the world,
it doesn't sound too different from home
and I see you hunched on darkened cliffs
looking out at more familiar waves.

You're here too. Hovering
between the lines of conversation
You're behind the concerned eyes
of my grandmother
as I pour the last glass and slip out,
just me
the waves
and red wine memories.

The sun sets the wrong way here,
even now it falls beneath the trees
leaving the ocean untouched and raging.

Uncle James

My Uncle is a very wise man,
he knows a lot of interesting things
but my favourite has always been
his passion for Harry Potter trivia.
We would sit for hours, each posing
the other a question until one of us
couldn't answer. It allowed a competitive streak
that neither of us could stretch in sports.
He always won, at least until the day
I learnt that Ollivander's was established in 382 BC.
Recently, I've been wanting to play again,
in a garden heavy with summer,
not to prove who is the biggest fan
but to talk about something other than death.

Little James

On the nights full of reasons
why we eventually left him,
you cried freely, barely
reached my waist.

At the funeral, you carried our father,
shouldered the coffin with men
who used to buy the drinks we later paid for,
You had something in your eye.

Now, you are so tall I can rest
my cheek against your chest, your chin
on my head; it's oddly comforting
squeezing your featherweight ribs.

Someone took a boy and stretched
too far, forced to grow
too fast so now I fear
you lack the needed bone density.

Over tea and cigarettes,
you tell me there is nothing
to grieve, you can't remember
anything but his forgetting.

Something Like Synaesthesia

You always sang tobacco brown
with burnt orange peels of filthy chuckles;
like the smell of the sea
or yesterday's bonfire.

You were not my only music teacher;
I built iridescence along the way—
painting the sound of light refracted
through glass or the feeling
of petals unfurling.

Today, I am singing the colour of fear
it is something like the smell of imminent
thunder or the tune of holding your breath
perhaps it has the tint of ash.

October the Sixth

They put him
               or the sand that was him
in a paper bag,
selloptaped closed
in what could have been a shoe box,
in a gift bag.
My sister put it—
             him
                   —on the back seat
did the seatbelt up— joked
safety first.

We originally planned
to do it on the cliff
but decided against it
when Granny said
she didn't want him
blowing down the beach
like a piece of rubbish,
so we waded into the sea.

I read somewhere that
they burn several bodies
at a time—
the beige dust you get
is not entirely your loved one.

We left them.
My father
the people he burned with
at the far end of the bay
in the rock pools.

My brother, sister and I
left our family—
                    his family
on the October sand.
The sea had lost its summer.

I wore the black T-shirt he bought me in Tennessee
Elvis has left the building.

Clutching the box
filled with our father
                    or the remains that were him,
we struggled with the Sellotape,
the sodden paper.
I wanted to laugh—
                    I think.
We unwrapped him—
                    it
like fish and chips.
Izzy held him—
                it
                    —up.

Go on then.
                    What?
Scoop him out then.

I got my father under my nails.
The wind caught him, threw him back.
I think I ate a bit.

Then it was over.
I tried not to think about baptism
as the sand that was ash
but was also my father,
ebbed.

Our congregation stood
at a respectful distance
inside winter coats.

We joined them,
falling to silence;
and the sea
      or the moment
           or the wind
              or grief
                  or the pressure to look like grief
          held us

until it didn't anymore.

It's Been a Year

It's been a year and you are still dead
and I am still trying to work out how I feel about that.

It's been 12 months and since you died
it took me 3 months to throw out
the McDonalds you left in my car.
I asked the man I love to marry me.
We are no closer to Brexit.
We planned your funeral.
I had 23 panic attacks.
We scattered your ashes.

It's been 52 weeks and I have written
an entire poetry collection;
taken a microscope to the you-shaped hole,
picked at the not-quite-healed scabs
to see what spilled out
on my notebook and made detailed notes.

It's been 365 days and I drink less now
I don't smoke at all
I don't miss the tar in my lungs
or the booze in my belly
burning and drowning
every night at the pub
even though I know that is what killed you.

It's been 8760 hours
I still don't know what I think about death
or where you might be right now.
I know that you are not here.
I know that the remains of the body
that was you but is now ash
have been scattered at the beach. Our beach—
right where you hosted my birthday parties.

Well-meaning Christians tell me
that you are in a better place
but if what they believe is true
then we both know you are not.

Some say that you live on in memories
and if they are right then there are any number of you:
the way your mother remembers,
the way my mother chooses to.
I would like to think that I've been faithful,
correct, in my many renderings.

It's been 525,600 minutes and I still miss you,
feel relieved that the shit show is over
still ache for the chance to fix us
I am beginning to realise,
I never could have fixed you anyway.

The Correct Spelling of Death is MAI

Mycobacterium avium-intracellulare
is an a-typical mycobacterial infection—
one with non-tuberculous mycobacteria.

More than a year later, when processing
the economic administration of death,
I learnt it was not Tuberculosis that killed him.

I try to find meaning in this discovery
but I do not know how
to pronounce the metaphor.

It doesn't sit right in my mouth
like lumps of infected mucus in lungs
scarred from a love affair with self-destruction.

This doesn't make any sense, so here are the facts:
Tuberculosis carried the weight of meaning with it
with images of women coughing into bloody tissues.

The terrifying heft of all that is gone
I need this to be important, I need
something to hold onto in this vacuum.

Dead Parent Club

Have one or more dead parents? Want to discuss funeral plans? Need advice on what probate is and how to do it witout fucking everything up? Fed up of making others uncomfortable with your emotions or new-found dark sense of humour? Just need to know if anyone else feels this way? Don't know what to feel but just need a pint with people who don't do the "head-tilt and sigh?" Join us! Topics of discussion include (but aren't limited to): selling belongings (how to shift those sledges you'll never use), bitching about other family members (maybe you love them, maybe you don't, no judgement here) bitching about the deceased, (don't worry, we won't tell them) bitching about how others treat you now and more! All are welcome. You don't have to have liked or even known your dead parent; just come along with an open heart and get a round in. We meet every Thursday at 8pm at The Hanging Man – we'll be the ones in the beer garden, listen for the laughter, or tears. For more information, please email deadparentclubpoetry@gmail.com

Viva Forever

Play this song at my funeral
with a slo-mo video montage of me
looking over my shoulder and laughing.

Think cheesy TV intros
Like *21 Jump Street, Buffy*
or the funeral from *Love Actually*.

Wear whatever you want;
comfort is a must,
sequins are optional but encouraged.

Play my playlist; the 10 hour one
which forged friendships
on cross-country car journeys.

Dance if you want.
Cry if you need.
Tell stories if you can.

Remember me for that time
I did that Justin Bieber tribute act
at the Student Union.

Remember me for Spyro fancy dress
or for getting us banned
from German jazz bars.

Remember me for all the excellent parties
and cuddly evenings in,
for cups of tea and mimosas.

Remember me smiling
Remember me for the Spice Girls
Remember me forever.

Grief as a Natural Disaster

When the water came
you didn't see it coming,
did not realise how close you were to the coast.
As your lungs filled
you thought the weight would crush you.

It didn't. You learnt
to live here, pulling oxygen from the sea.
You learnt to swim, grew
webbed hands and feet, evolved
amphibious. Eyes adapted to the dark.

You learnt to listen through echoes
to someone speaking with your voice.

When the water receded
you felt the sun burning
and clung to the retreating sea
until it left you too full
of panic.

You learnt to breathe
again, coughed out saltwater,
it's as painful as drowning;
legs used to swimming
learnt to hold
weight again.
You tried to speak. You didn't
recognise your waterlogged voice.

Their faces don't ripple
anymore, somehow it is harder
to focus— you realise
nothing you built
was ever waterproof.

Family Christmas

A few good friends and I were stranded in Bristol.
Father Christmas made each of us a stocking
and each brought their own traditions:
a tinselled tree surrounded by It's a Wonderful Life,
Frozen, Monopoly, Scrabble, stilton,
quiches, speeches, and own-brand brandy.

That night we played and talked and sipped,
loved and laughed late into the darkness
wrapped up in fairy lights and paper hats.
We were hodge-podged together,
the family we each chose
around a heavily laden, smiling table.

Charades

I am 27 years old and still feel the need to hide
from my mother-in-law at the end of her garden:

cracking leaves behind the shed under sensible sandals
as I sneak a lighter, breath out furtive fumes and hope
she thinks it's coming from next door even though
no one round here smokes nowadays.

Together, we preserve the charade
that I don't know that they know
that I know that they know
that I smoke.

I feel like a teenager again:
hiding below my Mum's living room window
sparking up and pretending.

I no longer hide from my mum.
At his funeral, she caught me in my weakness.
Since then, I've dropped all pretence of strength;
of any doubt that I am my Father's daughter.

But in this new family that I am yet to disappoint,
I slip out sneak behind the green house
spark up and pretend
to breathe easy.

Portrait of Widemouth Bay as Unending Apocalypse

They are planting Christmas trees
in Cornish sand dunes
to stop the ocean from reclaiming ground.

Far away ice is already melting,
she is rising with the heat
and a few misplaced trees will not stop her.

We try anyway,
in the hope that pines used to mountains
dig deep and find purchase
in the uncertainty of sand,
take root in a collection of broken things.

Five years came whiplash fast
the beach is a different shape now.
In the darkness of winter
we visit the spot we scattered him
raise toasts, give gifts, and decorate the branches.
We try our best to protect
the dying wood from the violence of wet,
try to stop the world moving quite so fast.

Father as Many Things

Breton-striped wife-beater vest,
a battered old camp-chair
with a beer holder,
a skinny, stray tomcat,
a swiss army knife with bottle opener
and no nail file, post-hippy
pre-punk, freak scene at 4:37 am
on a Friday night, the last
kebab he'd ever wake up to,
daytime repeats of crime dramas
to keep him company,
a garden shed full of tools with a rotted floor,
two-thirds saltwater, one-third gin,
a strong offshore wind sent
from a storm in the Atlantic,
thunder at a funeral,
a barbeque perfectly built in a kitchen sink.

Thank you, Father, ashes now,
for teaching me to build fires.

ACKNOWLEDGEMENTS

Thank you to Tim Liardet, Sophie Dumont, Nicola Heaney, and Anbur Ghouri who received my first drafts at their rawest and helped me turn them into poems.

Thank you to Bridget Hart and Suzannah Evans, editors who helped bash this collection into shape.

The truth is, this collection took five years to come into being and there are too many people to name who helped with that process. Thank you to my poetry pals in the Bristol poetry scene and beyond. Thank you to my family, friends in all the various group chats, and Treay. You all helped hold my scattered self in one piece through what has been a tough half decade.

Thanks to you reader, who picked up this book and gave my words your time, I am full of gratitude.

CREDITS

Thanks are due to the editors of the following publications in which some of these poems first appeared: *Ink, Sweat and Tears, Obsessed with Pipework, Stand Magazine, Flint the MA Creative Writing Anthology*, and *The Result Is What You See Today: Poems About Running – The Poetry Business Anthology*.

ABOUT VERVE POETRY PRESS

Verve Poetry Press is a quite new and already award-winning press that focused initially on meeting a local need in Birmingham - a need for the vibrant poetry scene here in Brum to find a way to present itself to the poetry world via publication. Co-founded by Stuart Bartholomew and Amerah Saleh, it now publishes poets from all corners of the UK - poets that speak to the city's varied and energetic qualities and will contribute to its many poetic stories.

Added to this is a colourful pamphlet series, many featuring poets who have performed at our sister festival - and a poetry show series which captures the magic of longer poetry performance pieces by festival alumni such as Polarbear, Matt Abbott and Imogen Stirling.

The press has been voted Most Innovative Publisher at the Saboteur Awards, and has won the Publisher's Award for Poetry Pamphlets at the Michael Marks Awards.

Like the festival, we strive to think about poetry in inclusive ways and embrace the multiplicity of approaches towards this glorious art.

www.vervepoetrypress.com
@VervePoetryPres
mail@vervepoetrypress.com